MORE
WEIRD THINGS
CUSTOMERS
SAY IN
BOOKSHOPS

MORE WEIRD THINGS CUSTOMERS SAY IN BOOKSHOPS

Jen Campbell

CONSTABLE

Constable & Robinson Ltd
55-56 Russell Square
London WC1B 4HP

This edition published by Constable,
an imprint of Constable & Robinson Ltd 2013

A copy of the British Library Cataloguing in Publication Data
is available from the British Library

ISBN-13: 978-1-47210-633-9 (hardback)
ISBN-13: 978-1-47210-741-1 (ebook)

Designed by Basement Press, Glaisdale
Printed and bound in the European Union

1 3 5 7 9 10 8 6 4 2

For bookshop customers, booksellers,
librarians, booklovers, book-hoarders,
bookworms and librocubicularists
(those who like to read in bed).

CONTENTS

The world of bookselling is anything but boring. In the past year a drunk man has thrown up on my shoes, a woman convinced herself I was hiding Hugh Grant in our storeroom, and a little girl tried to get to Narnia through one of our cupboards. And that's just the beginning.

Sometimes bookselling is the best job in the world. For example: a few months ago a customer gave us a call and said she was looking for a book she'd had as a child. She wanted to buy it to read to her grandchildren. As luck would have it, we had a copy, so we posted the book out to her. The following day, the customer called us back to say the book had arrived, and she couldn't believe it: it was her copy. Her copy of the book from when she was a child. It had the inscription on the frontispiece from her great aunt, and a bump to the spine where she'd accidentally dropped it when she was seven. Her mother had sold the book in a car boot sale forty years ago, two hundred miles away from our bookshop. Somehow, we'd come across it and, somehow, she'd happened to call us. Moments like that are just wonderful.

On a day to day basis, customers of all kinds make the bookselling world interesting. This book will show you the weird and wonderful side of that. The strange requests. The odd comments. The rude remarks. Not to mention the, quite frankly, amazingly awesome things children say – such as the boy who told me that, when he's older, he's going to become a book ninja. I have no idea what a book ninja is, but I want to hire that kid. Children are excellent.

Chatting to people about about *Weird Things Customers Say in Bookshops*, and travelling to other bookshops to talk about the book, has been a wonderful experience. I'm thrilled to be introducing the sequel. Like last time, this book also has quotes sent in from booksellers across the world, and there are some quotes from librarians, too. It's comforting (I think) to know that people are saying strange things everywhere.

Finally, this book has a little section at the back with some weird things said to me at *Weird Things...* book signings. Now there's a mouthful. Don't ask. Just read.

The other day, a customer asked me what my favourite 'weird thing' was. I told him that changed all the time, but I have a particular fondness for the person who asked if Anne Frank had written a sequel to her diary. The man laughed and said: 'You should have told her that she ghostwrote it!' I think I might love that customer.

Many thanks to the Twitter followers and bloggers who have come to visit Ripping Yarns after reading *Weird Things...* Special thanks to the two French guys who acted out scenes from the book in the middle of the shop – in French. Excellent stuff. And, seriously, to everyone who goes into bookshops – whether you happen to say weird things or not – thank you for supporting those bookshops.

Long live bookshops, their booksellers, and every single one of their customers. (Well, maybe not the guy who threw up on my shoes. Everyone else still counts.)

Jen Campbell

Ripping Yarns Bookshop

where I work, is an antiquarian bookshop in north London. Owned by Celia Mitchell, it's been a bookshop since the 1930s. We specialise in old children's books, but sell everything from biography and poetry to esoteric and ephemera.

◆

BOOKSELLER: Hi. Can I help you find anything?

CUSTOMER: Yes. This is your history section, right?

BOOKSELLER: Yep.

CUSTOMER: I can see you've got books on World War I and World War II.

BOOKSELLER: Yes, we do.

CUSTOMER: But I can't find any books on World War III. Where are those?

◆

CHILD: Mummy, who was Hitler?

MOTHER: Hitler?

CHILD: Yeah. Who was he?

MOTHER: Erm, he was a very bad man from a long time ago.

CHILD: Oh. How bad?

MOTHER: He was like … he was like Voldemort.

CHILD: Oh! That's really, really bad.

Mother: Yes.

CHILD: *(Pause)* So, did Harry Potter kill Hitler, too?

CUSTOMER *(picking up a copy of* Little Women*)*: Is this a book about really short people?

♦

CUSTOMER *(pondering)*: How much would a signed copy of the Bible be worth?
BOOKSELLER: Signed by whom?
CUSTOMER: Well … I don't know. Not God, obviously. *(Nervous laugh.)* That would be silly … wouldn't it?

♦

CUSTOMER: I'd like to return this *Where's Wally?* book, please.
BOOKSELLER: Why?
CUSTOMER: Because I've found him.

♦

CUSTOMER: Can you recommend a book of spells to raise pets from the dead?
BOOKSELLER: …
CUSTOMER: Just animals, you understand – not people. I don't want my husband coming back.

CUSTOMER: Do you make wanted posters for books?

BOOKSELLER: ... How do you mean?

CUSTOMER: I mean, can I bring you a list of books that I'm looking for, and then you could make them into wanted posters and put them up around the bookshop, in case other customers know where I could find them?

BOOKSELLER: Erm, I have a 'Wants' book that I can put your list of books in, and then I can let you know if we get those books in stock? Or I can try and track the books down for you myself, by calling other antiquarian booksellers?

CUSTOMER: No, that's OK. I like to pretend that the books are criminals, and that I'm tracking them down, like I'm the police. It's more fun that way.

BOOKSELLER: ... OK.

(Customer tries to walk out of the bookshop with a book that he hasn't paid for)
BOOKSELLER: Excuse me, you haven't paid for that book.
CUSTOMER: Yeah, I know. Don't worry; I'll bring it back tomorrow!

◆

CUSTOMER *(buying* Thirteen Ways to Dispose of a Dead Body, *whispers seriously)*: There are actually fourteen, you know.

◆

CUSTOMER: You've got a lot of books in here.
BOOKSELLER: Yep.
CUSTOMER: Do you ever just, like, sit here and count them?
BOOKSELLER: No, not really.
CUSTOMER: How long do you think it would take to count them all?
BOOKSELLER: A long time; we've got thousands and thousands of books.
CUSTOMER: How many exactly?
BOOKSELLER: … I don't know. I haven't counted.

◆

CUSTOMER: The Very Hungry Caterpillar was bulimic, right?

LITTLE GIRL *(pointing at* Dr. Seuss *books)*: I made a hat for my cat, but he won't wear it. That book is full of lies.

◆

CUSTOMER: Where would I find a book about William Shakespeare?
BOOKSELLER: We've probably got one in our biography section. I'll have a look for you.
CUSTOMER: Wouldn't it be in fiction? I mean, he wasn't a real person or anything, right?

CUSTOMER: I'm looking for this picture book for my daughter. I read about it in a review somewhere. I think it's by someone called E. L. James.

BOOKSELLER: Erm, I don't think it was by that person; that's who wrote *Fifty Shades of Grey*.

CUSTOMER *(going bright red and clutching her handbag, as though hiding something inside it)*: Oh! I don't know how that name cropped into my head, then. I've certainly never read any of those books! Never!

◆

CUSTOMER: Did they make a film edition of the Bible when *The Passion of the Christ* came out? You know, the text of the Bible, but with Mel Gibson on the front cover?

CUSTOMER: My Kindle's broken. Do you know how to fix it?
BOOKSELLER: I'm afraid Kindles aren't really my speciality.
CUSTOMER *(pulls her Kindle out of her bag)*: Look at it! I
dropped it in the bath!
BOOKSELLER: If you did that with a book, you could just
put it on the radiator and then flatten it out between two
heavier books.
CUSTOMER *(seriously)*: Do you think that would work for
this, too?

◆

CUSTOMER: Do you have a copy of this book but with the
title in red, instead of green? And maybe with a different
background image, too?
BOOKSELLER: … No.

◆

CUSTOMER *(holding up a book)*: What's this? *The Secret
Garden*? Well, it's not so secret now, is it, since they bloody
well wrote a book about it!

◆

CUSTOMER: Do you have a book on how to found countries?
I want to know if it's possible to claim my back garden as a
separate nation.

CUSTOMER: Do you have books on how to look after horses?
BOOKSELLER: Yep, they'll be in our nature section.
CUSTOMER: Great. I need to do research on how to look after unicorns, and they're basically the same thing.
BOOKSELLER: …

◆

(A customer is reading a book about the nativity)
CUSTOMER *(to her friend)*: Don't you ever get the feeling that Baby Jesus is somehow related to Herod? I always freak out, thinking that he's going to go: 'JESUS. I AM YOUR FATHER!'

CUSTOMER *(to her friend)*: You know the book *War Horse*?
CUSTOMER'S FRIEND: Yeah.
CUSTOMER: It's about horses during a war, right?
CUSTOMER'S FRIEND: Yeah, I think so.
CUSTOMER: But, like, how did they interview the horses to find out what it was like during the war?
CUSTOMER'S FRIEND: Dunno.
CUSTOMER *(clicks her fingers)*: Got it. Did they use a horse whisperer or something?
CUSTOMER'S FRIEND: I guess they must have done.
CUSTOMER: That's, like, so cool.

CUSTOMER: I'd love to write a book.

BOOKSELLER: Then you should write one.

CUSTOMER: I really don't have the time.

BOOKSELLER: I'm sure you could make time.

CUSTOMER: No, you don't get it; I really don't have the time. I had my fortune read on Monday, and the fortune teller lady said that I'm going to get knocked down by a bus next week. She said that it'll probably kill me.

BOOKSELLER: … Oh. Well, er, that doesn't sound very nice.

CUSTOMER: No, it doesn't, does it? It's really annoying, too, 'cause I'd booked a holiday for next month, and I was really looking forward to it.

◆

CUSTOMER: Ooh, books by Nicholas Shakespeare! Is he William Shakespeare's son?

CUSTOMER: I'd like a book for a friend about saving the world from alien invasion. I'd like the main character to be a little like Freddie Mercury and a little like Arnold Schwarzenegger. Does anything spring to mind?

CUSTOMER: Do you have *Windows 7 for Dummies*?
BOOKSELLER: Sorry, we're an antiquarian bookshop; nearly everything in here pre-dates computers.
CUSTOMER: Oh. Do you have user guides for antiquarian computers? You know from, like, the olden days, when they had swords and stuff?
BOOKSELLER: … ?

CHILD *(to bookseller)*: Does Santa come to your bookshop to get gifts for kids?
BOOKSELLER *(nodding wisely)*: Yes. Yes. He does.
CHILD: That's awesome!
BOOKSELLER: Yes, it is.
CHILD: But …
BOOKSELLER: But what?
CHILD: But … Santa's really fat. I don't think he could squeeze down the corridors between the bookshelves.
BOOKSELLER: It's OK. He sends us a list beforehand, and we leave the books by the door.
CHILD *(impressed)*: That makes you Santa's elf!
BOOKSELLER: Yes … yes, I suppose it does.

◆

CUSTOMER: Do you have any cards?
BOOKSELLER: We have some old postcards in a box by the door. Some of them have already been written on, though.
CUSTOMER: Oh, that's OK. Do you have one that says 'To Juliet, with love from Christine'? It would save me writing it out again, you see.

◆

CHILD: Mummy, where is the half-way point between Earth and Heaven? *(Pause)* It must be really far away. *(Pause)* Do you get to stop for a rest on your way up?

CUSTOMER: *Pride and Prejudice* was published a long time ago, right?

BOOKSELLER: Yep.

CUSTOMER: I thought so. Colin Firth's looking really good for his age, then.

◆

CUSTOMER: We're having a book burning at our religious group tonight. I need all your books on witchcraft.

BOOKSELLER: ...

CUSTOMER: And, as we're not going to read them, I expect a discount. We're doing the world a favour by burning them, you know.

◆

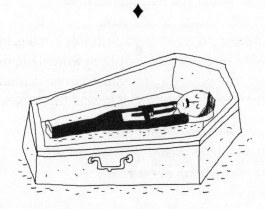

CUSTOMER: I don't like biographies. The main character pretty much always dies in the end. It's so predictable!

CUSTOMER *(with a French accent)*: Where is the cemetery?
BOOKSELLER: Oh, you go out of the bookshop and turn right …
CUSTOMER *(angrily)*: No, in French.
BOOKSELLER: Excuse me?
CUSTOMER: You tell me in French.
BOOKSELLER: … I don't speak French.
CUSTOMER *(outraged)*: You do not speak French?
BOOKSELLER: No. I can draw you a map, instead?
CUSTOMER: Non! Only in French!

◆

WOMAN *(holding a copy of a Weight Watchers book in one hand, and* The Hunger Games *in the other)*: Which of these dieting books would you recommend most?

◆

CUSTOMER *(to her friend)*: What do you do with your books after you've read them?
HER FRIEND: Sometimes I burn them.
CUSTOMER: You burn them?
HER FRIEND: Yeah. If I'm in the mood.

CUSTOMER: You know, I eat every good book I read.

BOOKSELLER: … Excuse me?

CUSTOMER: I like to feel as though the book's really part of me. So, when I've finished, I rip the pages up and put them in my food.

BOOKSELLER: What about the books you've read but don't like?

CUSTOMER: Well, obviously I don't eat those.

BOOKSELLER: Oh, yes, obviously. *(Pause)* What food goes best with paper?

CUSTOMER: Stews, mostly.

BOOKSELLER: I see.

CUSTOMER: And apple pie. That's good, too. But you must never make books into milkshakes. I tried that once and it was not nice at all.

BOOKSELLER: … I'll bear that in mind.

WOMAN: Last night I had a dream that your bookshop burnt down.

BOOKSELLER: Oh, well, thankfully we're still standing.

WOMAN: Well, just you be careful. I have a sense for these things, you see.

WOMAN'S HUSBAND: She does, you know. She had a premonition that her sister's house was going to be burgled.

WOMAN: That's right; I did. I warned her about it and everything, and did she believe me? No, she didn't.

WOMAN'S HUSBAND: Didn't believe her at all. And then, the next week, we went round to her sister's place to feed her cat when she was away, and we forgot to lock the back door and what do you know?

WOMAN: Boom!

BOOKSELLER: Boom?

WOMAN: Burgled.

BOOKSELLER: ... I see.

WOMAN: If only she'd listened to me. She could have stopped it from happening!

◆

CUSTOMER *(buying a copy of* Gulliver's Travels*)*: I'm thinking of going travelling, so I thought I'd give this a read to give me ideas of places to go. He seems to have gone to some really crazy parts of the world!

CUSTOMER: I really don't like the planet today – can you recommend a book set far, far away?

♦

CUSTOMER: I just baked a cake and I've burnt it all the way through. Look. *(She lifts a very burnt, blackened cake out of her bag.)* Do you have a book with instructions on how to fix it?

♦

YOUNG GIRL: Mummy, are the books on the top shelves only for really tall people?

YOUNG BOY: You should put a basement in your bookshop.

BOOKSELLER: You think so?

YOUNG BOY: Yeah. And then you could keep a dragon in it, and he could look after all the books for you when you're not here.

BOOKSELLER: That's a pretty cool idea. Dragons breathe fire, though. Do you think he might accidentally burn the books?

YOUNG BOY: He might, but you could get one who'd passed a test in bookshop-guarding. Then you'd be OK.

BOOKSELLER: You know, I think you're on to something there.

CUSTOMER: I'd like to buy this audiobook.

BOOKSELLER: Great.

CUSTOMER: Only, I don't really like this narrator.

BOOKSELLER: Oh.

CUSTOMER: Do you have a selection of narrators to choose from? Ideally, I'd like Benedict Cumberbatch.

CUSTOMER: Hi, I'm looking for a book, I was wondering if you could recommend one.

BOOKSELLER: Sure. Is it for you, or for a friend?

CUSTOMER: It's for me, dear. I was hoping to get a really good erotic novel, as an early birthday present to myself. Make bedtime reading that little bit more interesting, you know what I mean?

CUSTOMER: Personally, I think that if Jesus were alive today, he would go on a talent show and sing amazingly and win everyone over that way.

BOOKSELLER: … What would he sing?

CUSTOMER: Erm. That's a tough call. Probably a toss up between 'Imagine' and 'Saturday Night Fever.' Not because Jesus had a beard like John Lennon and the Bee Gees, but because I reckon he'd like us to feel spiritual but have a really good time, too.

◆

CUSTOMER *(holding up an art book)*: Wow. Picasso must have gone out with some really ugly women.

CUSTOMER: This is the bookshop from the film *Notting Hill*, isn't it?

BOOKSELLER: No, I'm afraid it's isn't.

CUSTOMER: It is. It looks exactly the same!

BOOKSELLER: Well, not really. The bookshop in *Notting Hill* is a travel bookshop. Also, it's in Notting Hill – the place.

CUSTOMER: You have a travel section, though.

BOOKSELLER: … Yes.

CUSTOMER: Are you not allowed to tell me that this bookshop is the one from the film, is that it?

BOOKSELLER: … We are not the bookshop from the film.

CUSTOMER: Oh *(winks)*. I see, I get it; you're not allowed to say. It's because you know Hugh Grant, right?

BOOKSELLER: … No. And Hugh Grant doesn't actually work in that bookshop; that was just for the film.

CUSTOMER: Aha! So you do know Hugh Grant!

BOOKSELLER: No, I–

CUSTOMER: Is he here? Is he in the back room?

BOOKSELLER: What? No!

CUSTOMER: It's OK, don't worry; I won't tell a soul.

◆

CUSTOMER *(to her friend)*: What about this book? *(holds up a copy of* The Hobbit*)*.

CUSTOMER: No. I don't want to read that. It'll spoil the film.

YOUNG BOY: When I grow up, I'm going to be a book ninja.
BOOKSELLER: Cool! What do book ninjas do?
YOUNG BOY: I can't tell you. It's top secret.

BOY *(picks up a copy of* Charlotte's Web *and holds it up to show his sister)*: What's this about?
GIRL: It's about a wimpy pig, and a spider called Charlotte who spins a web of lies and deceit.
BOOKSELLER: …

CUSTOMER *(to her friend)*: I only like books that I can really believe happened, you know? Like *Twilight*.

CUSTOMER: They should make vending machines for books. Then there'd be no more need for bookshops, and you could have a really long holiday. That'd be nice, wouldn't it?

◆

CUSTOMER: Are you prepared?
BOOKSELLER: ... For what?
CUSTOMER: For the zombie apocalypse.

(A woman is looking at a copy of Gone with the Wind*)*
HER SON: Is that a book about farts?

♦

CUSTOMER: Do you believe in past lives?
BOOKSELLER: Erm, well, I …
CUSTOMER: I do. I absolutely do. I feel very at one with everything. I'm pretty sure this is my seventh time on earth.
BOOKSELLER: I see.
CUSTOMER *(looking pleased with herself)*: And I'm almost certain that in a past life I was Sherlock Holmes.
BOOKSELLER: … You know, Sherlock Holmes is a fictional character.
CUSTOMER *(outraged)*: … Are you trying to tell me that I don't exist?
BOOKSELLER: …

♦

CUSTOMER: I'd like a Christmas book, about Christmas, that doesn't have anything to do with snow, or robins, or snowmen, or Jesus, or holly.
BOOKSELLER: … right.
CUSTOMER: And no bloody carols, either!

BOY *(reading titles of books on the shelf)*: *My Family and Other Animals*? Ha. Yes. I think my sister looks like a ferret.
HIS SISTER *(shouting from the other side of the shop)*: I heard that! And you look like a diseased baboon!

CUSTOMER: I'd like to buy a book for my wife.
BOOKSELLER: Sure, what sort of book?
CUSTOMER: I don't know. Something … pink? Women like pink stuff, right?

YOUNG GIRL *(pointing to a cupboard under one of the bookshelves)*: Can you get to Narnia through there?
BOOKSELLER: Unfortunately, I don't think you can.
YOUNG GIRL: Oh. Our wardrobe at home doesn't work for getting to Narnia, either.
BOOKSELLER: No?
YOUNG GIRL: No. Dad says it's because Mum bought it at IKEA.

◆

CUSTOMER: Have you read the Bible?
BOOKSELLER: Some parts.
CUSTOMER: I see. I think you should read all of it. I'm going to come to the bookshop once a week and read it aloud to you.
BOOKSELLER: That's really not necessary.
CUSTOMER: But I want to. I will read it to you in Italian, as that is my native tongue.
BOOKSELLER: … I don't understand Italian.
CUSTOMER: This does not matter.
BOOKSELLER: … I think it probably does.

◆

CUSTOMER: Do you have audiobooks on sign language?

CUSTOMER: Do you know anything about building small houses for chihuahuas?

◆

CUSTOMER: Do you have a copy of *The Handmaid's Tale*?
BOOKSELLER: I'm afraid we sold our copy of that this morning. I can order it in for you, though.
CUSTOMER: Can't you just print a copy for me? From the internet?

◆

CUSTOMER: What book do you recommend I read when I'm on the tube, to get girls to want to sleep with me?

YOUNG GIRL: Mummy, where do angels come from?
MOTHER: Erm …
YOUNG GIRL *(interrupting)*: I think they grow inside of clouds.
MOTHER: Oh, yes? How do you think they get there?
YOUNG GIRL: They come from eggs! That grow in space!
MOTHER: Interesting …

CUSTOMER: Do you hold cookery classes here?
BOOKSELLER: … No, we don't.
CUSTOMER: Oh. I was hoping to try out some of the recipes in your cookery books to see if they're any good.
BOOKSELLER: You'd have to buy a cookery book and try those recipes out at home.
CUSTOMER: Oh. Well. How very inconvenient.

CUSTOMER: There are several things I look for in a good book.

BOOKSELLER: Oh? What are those?

CUSTOMER: A murder – preferably of a handsome young man – a helicopter ride, a small dog, a parrot, a suicide, cigars, moustaches, love letters and animals that have escaped from the zoo.

BOOKSELLER: …

CUSTOMER: Why aren't you writing these things down?

BOOKSELLER: Sorry *(grabs a pen)*.

CUSTOMER: Good. Let's not forget the mysterious crop circles in the fields. Then there's the heroine – preferably a redhead from a country house in Wales, who collects fossils in her spare time. Her grandmother should be alive, but only just, and on the weekends she should ride wild horses on the beach. The heroine, that is, not the grandmother.

BOOKSELLER: … Right.

CUSTOMER: Any books spring to mind?

BOOKSELLER: No … It sounds like you should probably write this book yourself, considering you have such specific tastes.

CUSTOMER: You know, I rather hoped you might say that. *(He pulls a notebook out of his pocket.)* I've been outlining the story. Would you like to read it?

◆

CUSTOMER: I need a really awful book to give to someone I hate. Any recommendations?

(A young girl is looking at some pony books)
BOOKSELLER: Do you like horses?
YOUNG GIRL: Yes. When I grow up I'm going to have a pony.
BOOKSELLER: That sounds like fun.
YOUNG GIRL: Yes. And it will be better than all the other ponies.
BOOKSELLER: How come?
YOUNG GIRL: Because mine will have a purple tail. And roller-skates.

CUSTOMER: I don't like poetry. It seems so arbitrary. *(Pause)* Wait, that rhymes! Perhaps I'm an undiscovered poet.
BOOKSELLER: I thought you didn't like poetry?
CUSTOMER: Well, not other people's – but I would probably like my own!

CUSTOMER: Do you have this crime book? It's called *The Girl with the Dragon and the Baboon*?

CUSTOMER: What methods of payment do you accept?
BOOKSELLER: Cash, credit card, debit card, cheque …
CUSTOMER: Would you accept an IOU?

CUSTOMER *(whispers)*: Sometimes I think my cat is trying to kill me.
BOOKSELLER: Oh?
CUSTOMER: Only sometimes, though. Not all the time. Sometimes he can be quite nice.

LITTLE GIRL: Hello!

BOOKSELLER: Hi!

LITTLE GIRL: Guess where I'm going.

BOOKSELLER: Where?

LITTLE GIRL: My dad's taking me to the zoo!

BOOKSELLER: That sounds exciting.

LITTLE GIRL: Yes. It is. I want to read a book to the chimpanzees.

BOOKSELLER: You do?

LITTLE GIRL: Yes. Do you have a book with pictures of monkeys in it?

BOOKSELLER: I'm sure we do; I'll help you look.

LITTLE GIRL: Thanks. I think they'll like the pictures.

CUSTOMER: I'm looking for a white book.

BOOKSELLER: Do you know the title?

CUSTOMER: I'm not after a specific book – just a white one. I like things to look clean.

CUSTOMER: *(holding up a paperback)* If I buy this book, can I transfer it onto my friend's Kindle?

BOOKSELLER: … No.

CUSTOMER: Oh. How do they put physical books on a Kindle, then? Is it like that part in the film of *Charlie and the Chocolate Factory*, where Mike Teavee wants to become part of television, and he flies over everyone's heads in tiny little pieces?

CUSTOMER *(holding up an old, expensive book)*: Would you mind if I took the dust jacket from this? My copy doesn't have a jacket, you see.

BOOKSELLER: You mean you want to buy the dust jacket?

CUSTOMER: No, I don't want to buy it. I just want to have it. Do you have a problem with that?

CUSTOMER: Tell me, is *Harry Potter and the Philosopher's Stone* still in print?

BOOKSELLER: Yes, of course.

CUSTOMER: I wasn't sure if they stopped printing it, you see – surely everyone has a copy by now?

CUSTOMER: I've got a list of books for my son's GCSE English class. Can you check if you have them?

BOOKSELLER: Sure, what are they?

CUSTOMER *(reading from the list)*: The first one is *Jane Eyre Laid Bare*.

BOOKSELLER: Erm, I'm pretty sure that he just needs *Jane Eyre* by Charlotte Brontë.

CUSTOMER: No. That's not the title written down here. This one's written by Charlotte Brontë and someone else. I suppose it must be some sort of literary criticism?

BOOKSELLER: … Erm, well, *Jane Eyre Laid Bare* is erotica – a retelling of the novel.

CUSTOMER: Oh. That can't be right. Wait a minute, and I'll call him.

(Customer phones her son)

CUSTOMER: Hi David … yes … I'm just getting your course books and this woman here is telling me that *Jane Eyre Laid Bare* is some sort of erotic novel. That's not right, is it? Do you know what she's talking about?

(Pause)

CUSTOMER *(hissing angrily down the phone)*: What do you mean you thought you'd just read that one instead?

CUSTOMER: What's so great about *The Great Gatsby*, anyway? Was he a superhero or something?

MOTHER: Henry! Stop chewing that book. You don't know where it's been.

CHILD: No!

MOTHER *(rolling her eyes at the bookseller)*: Kids, ey? *(She wanders off and her son continues to chew the book.)*

CUSTOMER *(seriously)*: Your window display's not very friendly. It's got stuff on ghosts, and haunted houses and poltergeists and everything. Are you trying to scare your customers away?

BOOKSELLER: … No, sir. It's Hallowe'en.

(A man runs through the door, out of breath)
MAN: Hi. My friends and I were playing cricket in the park, and it's started raining.
(Man looks at bookseller expectantly)
BOOKSELLER: … ?
MAN *(impatiently)*: Well, I was wondering if we could finish our game in your bookshop?
BOOKSELLER: … You want to play cricket … in the bookshop?
MAN: Yeah!
BOOKSELLER *(glancing around at the tiny shop, crammed full of books)*: Erm, there's really no room … at all.
MAN: Well, we only need one aisle between the shelves, really. And we could always move the bookcases.
BOOKSELLER: … I'm going to have to say no. It would be dangerous, and I don't think the other customers would like it.
MAN: Oh, come on. They could cheerlead or something.
BOOKSELLER: … No.
MAN: And you could be the umpire!
BOOKSELLER: … No.
MAN: I promise we wouldn't break too many things.
BOOKSELLER: … No.

CHILD *(outside bookshop)*: Mummy, can we go inside the bookshop?
MOTHER: Not now. You're too young. You can go in when you're older.

CUSTOMER: You never read about Middle Earth any more, do you? It's like no one cares about The Shire these days. Stuff must still happen there but it's never reported in the news.

CUSTOMER'S FRIEND: They're making new movies, aren't they?

CUSTOMER: Are they?

CUSTOMER'S FRIEND: Yeah, but I think it's like a history. It's not what's happening there now. That's what I heard.

CUSTOMER: So what's happening there now?

CUSTOMER'S FRIEND: I don't know. Let's look it up on Wikipedia when we get home.

CUSTOMER: Good idea.

♦

CUSTOMER: Do you have any hollowed out books?

BOOKSELLER: You mean fake books? The kind people use as a safe place?

CUSTOMER: Yeah. But with stuff already in them.

BOOKSELLER: No, we don't.

CUSTOMER: 'Cause people use them to hide all sorts of stuff, don't they? Drugs … guns. Do you have a fake book with a gun in it?

BOOKSELLER: … No.

CUSTOMER: Oh. Do you know where I could get a gun without the fake book?

BOOKSELLER: … No, I don't.

CUSTOMER: I'm looking for books for an eight-year-old girl. What would you recommend?

BOOKSELLER: Well, is she a confident reader for her age?

CUSTOMER: Yes.

BOOKSELLER: And what are her interests?

CUSTOMER: Horses, princesses, dancing …

BOOKSELLER: OK – I'll help you find some.

(Bookseller spends the next ten minutes finding books for the customer, talking about each one in turn.)

CUSTOMER: Great. Thanks. I'll bear all those in mind.

BOOKSELLER: Would you like us to keep any on reserve for you?

CUSTOMER *(gets out pen and paper to write down the titles)*: No, I'll just write them down. I don't want them myself. I'm writing a book, you see, about an eight year old girl and I wanted to work out what books she should have on her bookcase.

BOOKSELLER: So you don't want to buy any?

CUSTOMER: Oh, no dear. Don't be silly. I might have the character purchase some of the books in the story itself. But not in real life.

BOOKSELLER: … I see.

CUSTOMER: And, to be honest, my character's rather advanced for her age with regard to technology. So I might have her buy them online instead.

BOOKSELLER: … Right.

(Bookseller sees a customer putting some garlic on a bookshelf)
BOOKSELLER: ... Er, excuse me, can I ask what you're doing?
CUSTOMER: These books are about vampires. I'm taking precautions.

CUSTOMER *(bursts into the shop)*: You haven't seen my ferret have you?
BOOKSELLER: No, I can't say I have.
CUSTOMER: Right, well, if you do see him, please keep him safe.
BOOKSELLER: ... Will do.

CUSTOMER: Can I pay with an Amazon gift card?

♦

CUSTOMER: How many Sickles are there to a pound?
BOOKSELLER: I don't know, why?
CUSTOMER: I want to set up an underground currency.

♦

CUSTOMER *(going through comics)*: Pfft. Look at all these so-called superheroes. Spiderman bitten by a spider, The Hulk getting all radioactive. I was bitten by my sister's hamster when I was five but you don't hear me going on about it!

LITTLE BOY *(whispers)*: You should stock up on food.
BOOKSELLER: Should I?
LITTLE BOY: Yes.
BOOKSELLER: Why?
LITTLE BOY *(seriously)*: The aliens are coming.
BOOKSELLER: … They are?
LITTLE BOY: Yes. ET is angry, and he wants revenge!

◆

CUSTOMER: I can't afford a gym membership. Would you mind if I came in here three or four times a week? I'd like to use your larger books to do some weight-lifting.

CUSTOMER: They say there's a book inside all of us, don't they?

BOOKSELLER: … They do say that.

CUSTOMER: How do I find mine? I think it's hiding from me.

BOOKSELLER: … I don't think you can really rush these things.

CUSTOMER *(muttering to herself)*: I need a book x-ray. That's what I need.

◆

CUSTOMER: Do bookshops have talking books for hire?

BOOKSELLER: Well, we have audiobooks that you can buy.

CUSTOMER: No, that's not what I mean. I don't want a CD. I want a person. Someone who has learnt a book off by heart and will come to my house to read it out to me.

BOOKSELLER: … You mean like in *Fahrenheit 451*?

CUSTOMER: I don't know what that is. I just want someone to come to my house and recite a book to me.

BOOKSELLER: We don't offer services like that, I'm afraid.

CUSTOMER: Well, if you ever do, please let me know.

◆

CUSTOMER: I had such a crush on Captain Hook when I was younger. Do you think this means I have unresolved issues?

(Phone rings)
BOOKSELLER: Hello, Ripping Yarns bookshop.
CUSTOMER: Hi, am I speaking to a bookseller?
BOOKSELLER: You are indeed.
CUSTOMER: Great. Listen, I need you to help me with this crossword …

◆

LITTLE BOY: Do you have any superpowers?
BOOKSELLER: Sadly, I don't think I do. Do you?
LITTLE BOY *(whispers)*: Yes. I can fly. But only when no one else is watching.

◆

CUSTOMER: Am I your ten thousandth customer?
BOOKSELLER: … I don't think so.
CUSTOMER: Oh. Damn. I thought that, if I was, you might give me a prize. Hmmm. I'll come back later.

◆

CUSTOMER: Where's your Amazon section?
BOOKSELLER: … Are you looking for a book about the Amazon river?
CUSTOMER *(exasperated)*: No. Not the river. Amazon. You know? Online. Where's your section of books from there?

CUSTOMER: Where are your books on war?
BOOKSELLER: They'll be in with history. Our history section is split up into British History, European History, American History and World History. Which war are you looking for, specifically?
CUSTOMER: I want a history of the ongoing war between werewolves and vampires.
BOOKSELLER: ...
CUSTOMER: Where would I find that?

CUSTOMER: I want to get my girlfriend a book for her birthday but I don't know if she already has it.
BOOKSELLER: OK.
CUSTOMER: Could you find out for me?
BOOKSELLER: ... How?
CUSTOMER: Well, maybe you could call her and say that you're doing a survey or something?
BOOKSELLER: ...
CUSTOMER: You know, just lie and gain her trust and find out everything you can.

(It's the end of the day, the lights are off in the bookshop, the closed sign is up. The bookseller is by the door, about to lock up, when a lady hurries into the shop)

BOOKSELLER: Hi, I'm sorry but we're closed.

LADY: What? I'm on the phone *(points to her phone)*.

BOOKSELLER: OK, but I'm afraid we're closed.

LADY *(into the phone)*: One sec, Mary. *(She turns to the bookseller, annoyed)* That's OK; I don't want any books, I just want to talk on the phone; it's too loud outside.

BOOKSELLER: I'm sorry but I really have to leave now; you'll have to speak on the phone somewhere else.

LADY *(curtly)*: You can just wait a minute while I finish my call. *(Into the phone)* Sorry about that, Mary … Yes, just some stupid girl who doesn't want me to talk to you … Anyway, yes, as I was saying, I think we should probably get the blue sofa; it'll match the wallpaper nicely …

CUSTOMER: Do you have a Christmas book about that, like, really famous baby?

CUSTOMER: Do you have any books signed by authors who are likely to die very soon? I'd like to make an investment.

CUSTOMER *(to her daughter)*: What kind of book would you like, sweetie?

LITTLE GIRL: I'd like a book with cats and cows and dogs and geese and horses and antelopes AND centipedes, because they're ALL my friends.

CUSTOMER: This book looks good. How can I watch it?

BOOKSELLER: Excuse me?

CUSTOMER: Where's the film? Is it tucked inside the cover or something?

CUSTOMER *(holding up a £25 book)*: Can I make you an offer of £1 for this book?

BOOKSELLER: … You can, but I won't accept it.

CUSTOMER: This book's in Russian; you're not going to sell it.

BOOKSELLER: We have some Russian customers and collectors, and that book is rare.

CUSTOMER: But I don't speak Russian – so I'm not going to pay £25 for it!

BOOKSELLER: … If you don't speak Russian, then why do you want it?

CUSTOMER: I don't know … It sort of looks nice.

CUSTOMER: My son's getting married next week. Do you have a book to help me make sure it doesn't rain on his big day? Some incantations or something?

(Drunken man bursts through the door, and stumbles inside)

DRUNKEN MAN *(looking around in amazement)*: Dude. Your bookshop is, like, totally moving.

BOOKSELLER: …

DRUNKEN MAN: … Like, sideways. And in circles!

LITTLE GIRL: Hello. I've asked for lots of books for Christmas.
BOOKSELLER: That's great! Books are wonderful presents.
LITTLE GIRL: Yes. I've written them all down in a list for Santa.
MOTHER: That's right. Remember, when you've finished writing that list, give it to me and I'll make sure Santa gets it.
LITTLE GIRL: It's OK; I've already posted it.
MOTHER: ... What?
LITTLE GIRL: I posted it on the way home from school.
MOTHER: ... In the postbox?
LITTLE GIRL: Yeah! I didn't know all of his address, but I'm sure he'll find it. I'm excited!
MOTHER: ...

◆

LITTLE BOY: Look! Peter Rabbit!
FATHER: Rabbits belong in pies, son. Not in books.

CUSTOMER *(whilst paying for a book)*: I have always wanted to marry a bookseller.
(Pause)
CUSTOMER: Do you fantasise about marrying one of your customers?
BOOKSELLER: ...

◆

(Customer walks into the bookshop and looks around admiringly)
CUSTOMER: I love old bookshops.
BOOKSELLER: Thank you.
CUSTOMER: I always think I might find something really good in them. You know, like a treasure chest owned by Victorian pirates. That'd be pretty cool.

(Phone rings)
BOOKSELLER: Hello, Ripping Yarns Bookshop.
CUSTOMER: Hi, am I talking to a real person?
BOOKSELLER: Yep.
CUSTOMER: Not a recording machine?
BOOKSELLER: … No.
CUSTOMER: Prove it!

◆

CUSTOMER: I'm bored. Can you recommend something for me?
BOOKSELLER: Sure, what kind of books do you like to read?
CUSTOMER: I don't want to read a book! Didn't you hear what I said? I'm BORED. I need something INTERESTING to do!

◆

CUSTOMER: Urgh. Shakespeare. He's everywhere, isn't he? You can't escape him. I wish he'd do us all a favour and just die already.

◆

CUSTOMER: I'm looking for a book on the war of 1066.
CUSTOMER'S FRIEND: When was that?

CUSTOMER: How much are your books?

BOOKSELLER: The prices are written in pencil inside each book.

CUSTOMER: But how much are they?

BOOKSELLER: They're all different prices.

CUSTOMER: Why? They're basically the same.

BOOKSELLER: Well–

CUSTOMER *(interrupting)*: They're all made of paper! They all have words!

LITTLE GIRL: I read a book last week called *What Katy Did.*

BOOKSELLER: Did you like it?

LITTLE GIRL: It was OK. I didn't think it was very realistic, though. My name is Katy, and I haven't done any of the things that the girl in the book has done.

CUSTOMER *(Holding up a nineteenth century edition of* Oliver Twist*)*: Where's the barcode on this? I want to price check it on my smart phone.

BOOKSELLER: … Barcodes didn't exist back then.

CUSTOMER: Oh. Well, how am I supposed to find out if I can buy it cheaper somewhere else then?

BOOKSELLER: …

CUSTOMER: Could you look it up for me on your computer?

CUSTOMER: *The Sheep-Pig?* Is that some kind of mutant?

(A mother and her little boy come into the bookshop)
LITTLE BOY *(looking around, astounded)*: Mummy ... have we gone back in time?!

CUSTOMER: I'm looking for a birthday present for a friend. She loves books.
BOOKSELLER: Great, I can help you look if you want?
CUSTOMER: Thanks. Oh, wait! Do you do birthday cakes shaped like books? She'd love that!
BOOKSELLER: ... No.
CUSTOMER: OK. What do you do?
BOOKSELLER: We do books ... shaped like books.
CUSTOMER: Ah. OK. That could work, too.

CUSTOMER: I'd like to talk to you about God.

BOOKSELLER: I'm sorry but I don't discuss religion with our customers.

CUSTOMER: Are you denying God? God could be anywhere! What if I'm God – do you risk denying me?

(Pause)

CUSTOMER *(glaring angrily)*: God's everywhere, lady! He's probably hiding behind this bookcase!

CUSTOMER: I need to return this book *(produces* The Iron Man *by Ted Hughes)*.

BOOKSELLER: Is there a problem?

CUSTOMER: Yes! It doesn't have Robert Downey Jr. in it. AT ALL.

WOMAN: I think my grandson has swallowed a love potion. Do you have a book that has an antidote?
BOOKSELLER: Why do you think he's swallowed a love potion?
WOMAN: He's completely besotted with a girl who is not good enough for him. Not good enough at all!
BOOKSELLER: ...
WOMAN: I didn't really believe in love potions myself, you know, but now I'm not so sure.
BOOKSELLER: I see.
(Pause)
WOMAN *(angrily)*: Kids! They've got all sorts of ideas in their heads these days. It's all because of that Harry Potter!

CUSTOMER *(looking at the history section)*: I've always wanted to be a prisoner of war.
BOOKSELLER: ...
CUSTOMER: It sounds romantic, doesn't it?

CUSTOMER: I'm looking for that book … *Romeo and Juliet*. It's about a fight between the DiCaprios and another gang. Street stuff.
CUSTOMER'S FRIEND: Yeah. It's the true story of Leonardo DiCaprio.

◆

CUSTOMER: I'd like to buy a book for a friend.
BOOKSELLER: Sure, what does she like?
CUSTOMER *(deep in thought)*: Well, she's quite racist …
BOOKSELLER: …

◆

CUSTOMER *(eagerly)*: I really liked *Fifty Shades of Grey*. *(Pause)* Do you have an illustrated version?

◆

LITTLE GIRL *(with her hands on her hips, talking about* Alice in Wonderland*)*: Alice falls down a hole in the ground because she doesn't look where she's going? I wouldn't be that stupid.

◆

CUSTOMER: Are these books fire-proof?
BOOKSELLER: … Nope.
CUSTOMER: Well, that's not very useful is it?

(Phone rings)
BOOKSELLER: Hello?
CUSTOMER: Oh, you're there! Thank goodness.
BOOKSELLER: How can I help?
CUSTOMER: I'm making a chicken pie from handwritten instructions, and I can't read my own handwriting.
BOOKSELLER: ... Right.
CUSTOMER: Could you check the recipe for me?
Bookseller: ... How?
CUSTOMER: Oh! I copied it out of one of the books on the top shelf of your cookery section when I was in last week. I write a new one down whenever I come in – no point in buying the whole book when I can just do that. I was in a hurry last time so my writing's a mess!
BOOKSELLER: ...
CUSTOMER: I need to know what happens after I add the stock. Could you have a look? It's the big black book, with gold lettering on the spine.
BOOKSELLER: I'm afraid I sold that book earlier today.
CUSTOMER: What? But ... but I need it! Why didn't you stop them taking it?

♦

CUSTOMER: Do you have a book on how to identify swingers?

CHILD: What's your oldest book?
BOOKSELLER: We have a set of books from 1776.
CHILD: Wow ... That's nearly as old as grandma!

CUSTOMER: Do you have any audiobooks in Chinese? I want them for my six year old son.
BOOKSELLER: I don't think we do. Does your son speak Chinese?
CUSTOMER: No.
BOOKSELLER: ... Are you looking for an audiobook to help him learn Chinese?
CUSTOMER: He doesn't need to learn it; I just want a story in Chinese for him to listen to.
BOOKSELLER: But ... how will he understand it?
CUSTOMER *(frustrated)*: Look, there's a billion people who can understand Chinese on this planet. Are you saying my son is stupid?

CUSTOMER: Do you have a copy of *Jane Eyre*? We're doing it in our book club.

BOOKSELLER: Sure. I'll just get you a copy.

CUSTOMER: Thanks. You know, I go to this book club thing, but I really hate reading.

BOOKSELLER: So ... why do you go to the book club?

CUSTOMER: I don't know, really. *(Pause)*. To make things easier, I bought a book called *How To Talk About Books You Haven't Read*.

BOOKSELLER: Yeah?

CUSTOMER: Yeah. *(Pause)*. I didn't read it.

◆

CUSTOMER: I bought this book last week, and I'd like to return it.

BOOKSELLER: I just saw you pick this book up from the shelf and bring it to the desk. You didn't buy it last week.

CUSTOMER *(looking shifty)*: I did!

BOOKSELLER: ... No, you didn't.

CUSTOMER: ... OK. Fine. I didn't.

BOOKSELLER: So, can you put the book back on the shelf?

CUSTOMER *(angrily)*: Wait a minute; I might want to buy it. Don't jump to conclusions!

◆

CUSTOMER: Do you have *Harry Potter and the Prisoner of Abracadabra*?

CUSTOMER: I'd like to buy these books using this voucher.
BOOKSELLER: … Erm, this voucher is for a free burger.
CUSTOMER: Yes. I thought it should be a ratio of two books to one burger. Does that seem fair?

◆

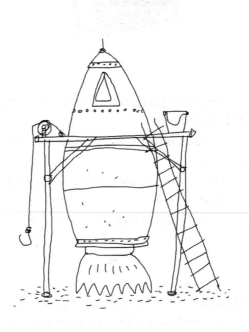

CUSTOMER: Guess what.
BOOKSELLER: What?
CUSTOMER: I'm building a spaceship in my back garden to scare my neighbours.

LITTLE GIRL: I want to play hide and seek. Do you have a big book that I can hide in?

BOOKSELLER: Not a book, but we could hide behind a bookcase?

LITTLE GIRL: But ... but, mum says she likes books because you can get lost in them.

BOOKSELLER: Ah, I don't think that's quite what she meant.

(Door bangs open and a flustered looking man runs in)

FLUSTERED LOOKING MAN: I'm the idiot who tried to get in earlier when you were closed! Did you see me? I literally tried to open the door for two whole minutes! Did you notice?

BOOKSELLER: Well ... no ... because we were closed ... and I wasn't here.

Weird Things Customers Say in Other Bookshops

(and libraries, too!)

♦

CUSTOMER: Excuse me, where do you keep all your books?
BOOKSELLER: … They're all around you.
CUSTOMER: Oh. Right. I see.

Iida Henriksson: *Suomalainen Kirjakauppa, Finland.*

◆

CUSTOMER: Do you work here?
BOOKSELLER: Yes.
CUSTOMER: Oh, good. I couldn't tell if you were wearing a uniform or you just really liked Waterstones.

◆

CUSTOMER *(pointing at the books on the shelves)*: Are these real books?
BOOKSELLER: … Yes.
CUSTOMER: So, they're not e-books? They're real? I can look at them?
BOOKSELLER: … Yes.

CUSTOMER: Excuse me, I hid a book down the back of that bookshelf yesterday, but I can't seem to find it today.
BOOKSELLER: I'm afraid I sold that. I found it last night when I was tidying up.
CUSTOMER: What did you do that for? I wanted to buy that!
BOOKSELLER: If you want to reserve something, you should ask us to keep it behind the till instead of hiding it behind a bookshelf.
(Customer storms off)

◆

CUSTOMER: Who wrote *Paradise Lost*?
BOOKSELLER: John Milton.
CUSTOMER: No, that's not it.
BOOKSELLER: Yes, it was him.
CUSTOMER: And how would you know?

Jennifer Burt: *Waterstones, Plymouth Drake Circus, UK.*

◆

(Elderly female customer is looking at the chart)
CUSTOMER: I can't believe everybody's reading this *Fifty Shades* …
BOOKSELLER: I know. I take it it isn't your cup of tea, then?
CUSTOMER: Oh, no dear; been there, done that – no need to read about it!

Joe Giaffreda: *Waterstones, Peterborough, UK.*

CUSTOMER *(in a broad Northern Irish accent)*: Do you have the book *Landscapes of War*?
BOOKSELLER: No, we're actually a religious bookshop.
CUSTOMER: Oh, is that what you are?
BOOKSELLER: Yes, you'd be better off trying one of the other bookshops in town.
CUSTOMER: Oh, right.
(Pause)
CUSTOMER: Do you have that book all them women are reading?
BOOKSELLER: Ahem …

Richard Ryan: *The Good Book Shop, Belfast, UK.*

(A customer has brought in a box of coverless, very damaged books and wants the bookshop to buy them)
BOOKSELLER: I'm sorry madam, but we don't buy books like this.
CUSTOMER: But your sign says that you buy books, and I want to get rid of these. What sort of books do you buy?
BOOKSELLER: Well, perhaps the sort of books you left at home?
CUSTOMER: I wouldn't want to sell those! They're nice books!

Ian Snelling: *SA Book Connection, KwaZulu-Natal, South Africa.*

CUSTOMER: Do you have a book that interprets life?
BOOKSELLER: I'm not sure I know what you mean.
CUSTOMER: Well, I was out hiking the other day, and I saw a wolf. I want to know what that meant.

Jody Mosley: *Barnes and Noble, Boulder, Colorado, USA.*

CUSTOMER: Can you recommend something to read? I'm very widely read.
BOOKSELLER: Sure, how about–
CUSTOMER *(interrupting)*: I don't read anything written in the first person.
BOOKSELLER: OK, how about–
CUSTOMER: And I don't read books by women. I just can't stand things written by female authors.

Tilly Lunken: *Thesaurus Books, Melbourne, Australia.*

CUSTOMER: Do you have a true crime section?

BOOKSELLER: Yes.

(Bookseller takes customer to the true crime section.
A few minutes later, the customer moves towards the front door
with a book in his pocket.)

BOOKSELLER: Erm, are you going to pay for that book?

CUSTOMER: No.

BOOKSELLER *(taking book from customer's pocket)*: Please don't come back.

CUSTOMER: Oh. Does this mean I have to bring all the other books back, too?

BOOKSELLER: …

Toby Halsey: *Elizabeth's Bookshops, Perth, Australia.*

(While browsing our antiquarian section, a customer drops a 160 year old book. The marbled front end board cartwheels in the opposite direction to the text block as it hits the floor. With her hand to her chest, the customer gasps, looks at the book, then sighs with relief)

CUSTOMER: Gosh, thank goodness that was just some old book!

James Findlay: *Explorers Books, Johannesburg, South Africa.*

CUSTOMER: Hi, I'm looking for a book version of my Sat Nav.

BOOKSELLER: … Do you mean a road map?

CUSTOMER: … Maybe.

Stephanie Ose: *Waterstones, Newbury, UK.*

LITTLE GIRL: Mommy, I could stay in here all day!

MOTHER: I don't know why you read; it'll never get you anywhere.

MAN *(looking at a giant map in the bookstore)*: When did they move New Zealand way down by Australia? Wasn't it in Europe before?
BOOKSELLER: …

♦

CUSTOMER: These are used books?
BOOKSELLER: Yes
CUSTOMER: Do you have the Stephen King book that comes out next week?
BOOKSELLER: … No.

♦

(One bright Saturday afternoon)
CUSTOMER *(walks up to counter)*: Are you open on Saturdays?

Christopher Sheedy: *Re:Reading Bookstore, Toronto, Canada.*

BOOKSELLER: Would you like a bag?
CUSTOMER: No, I'd like a divorce.

Georgine Balassone: *Bookshop Santa Cruz, California, USA.*

CUSTOMER *(anxiously, to friend)*: I don't know where it'd be; I have no idea what section it would be in. I just don't know.
BOOKSELLER: Hello, do you need any help?
CUSTOMER *(annoyed)*: No, we're fine, thank you.

◆

WOMAN: Do you have any books about sexual health?
BOOKSELLER: Yes, in the health section just behind me.
WOMAN: Because you can never be too careful nowadays, can you?
BOOKSELLER: I guess not.
WOMAN: It's always good to be prepared, isn't it?
BOOKSELLER: Yes, of course.
WOMAN: Protection is very important.
BOOKSELLER: … Yep.
WOMAN: Are you always prepared? What do you normally use for protection?
BOOKSELLER: …

◆

BOOKSELLER: As you've spent over ten pounds, you could buy a copy of *The Host* by Stephenie Meyer for just one pound ninety nine?
CUSTOMER: Oh no. I'd never read a book written by a Mormon.

Nicholas Blake: *Waterstones, Nottingham, UK.*

CUSTOMER *(looking at a full wall of shelves dedicated to Shakespeare)*: Is that all the Shakespeare you have in stock?
BOOKSELLER: Yes, but I can order anything specific if we don't have it.
CUSTOMER: Well, I think it's disgraceful that you seem to have all of his plays and none of his novels.

Tracey Sinclair: *University Bookshop, Glasgow, UK.*

◆

CUSTOMER: In which section would I find a book on the workings of the internal combustion engine, suitable for a three-year-old?

◆

CUSTOMER *(holding a signed copy of a Jacqueline Wilson book)*: I want to buy this book, but not this copy because someone's written in it.
BOOKSELLER: … That's the author's signature.
CUSTOMER: I don't care who's written in it – I just want a clean copy!

Clare Poole: *PG & Wells Booksellers, Winchester, UK.*

CUSTOMER: Where's your true fiction section?

Betsy Urbik: *Barnes and Noble, Rockford, Illinois, USA.*

CUSTOMER: Do you have *Harry Potter* book seven, part two?
BOOKSELLER: Book seven, *The Deathly Hallows*, is just one volume.
CUSTOMER: But the movie has two parts, so there must be a second book! They don't just make movies from nothing!

Gabe Konrád: *Bay Leaf Used & Rare Books, Sand Lake, Michigan, USA.*

CUSTOMER: Have you read …
BOOKSELLER: …
CUSTOMER: Oh, never mind. You look too young to have read a good book.

Madison Butler: *Liberty Bay Books, Poulsbo, Washington, USA.*

CUSTOMER: I'm looking for a book called *I Know Why the Care Bear Sings*.

Liz Scott: *Waterstones, Bradford, UK.*

CUSTOMER: Do you have any blank books?
BOOKSELLER: You mean like a journal?
CUSTOMER: No, a real book, just blank.

Erica Hensley: *Bound To Be Read Books, Atlanta, Georgia, USA.*

◆

CUSTOMER: This *Abraham Lincoln: Vampire Hunter* book has to be the most historically accurate fiction book I've read.

Carrie Austin: *Island Bookstore, Kitty Hawk, North Carolina, USA.*

◆

CUSTOMER: Can you help me find a book, please?
BOOKSELLER: Sure, what are you in the mood for?
CUSTOMER *(leaning in very closely)*: I'm feeling very vulnerable right now.

Meaghan Beasley: *Island Bookstore, Kitty Hawk, North Carolina, USA.*

(Phone rings)

CUSTOMER: Hello. I'm looking for a first edition of *The Sun Also Rises* by Ernest Hemingway.

BOOKSELLER: I'm sorry, sir, but we don't stock secondhand or rare books.

CUSTOMER: I don't want a secondhand copy! I want a new one!

BOOKSELLER: Sir, the first edition of this book was published in 1926.

CUSTOMER: I don't want one that old!

BOOKSELLER: But–

(Customer hangs up)

Karen T. Brissette: *Barnes and Noble, Union Square, New York, USA.*

CUSTOMER: I would like to buy a book called *Never Let You Go*.

BOOKSELLER: Do you mean *Never Let Me Go*, by Kazuo Ishiguro? *(holds up a copy of the book)*

CUSTOMER: No. The book I'm looking for is by Kazuo Ishiguro but it's definitely called *Never Let You Go*, not *Never Let Me Go*.

BOOKSELLER: …

CUSTOMER: He must have written two books with very similar titles. I'd be grateful if you could track the other one down for me.

Jefth Chan: *One Page Bookshop, Hong Kong.*

BOOKSELLER: Can I help you find anything?

WOMAN: Yes. We're looking for the portal.

BOOKSELLER: ... Sorry?

MAN: We're looking for the portal.

BOOKSELLER: ...

WOMAN: We've been tracking the portal to Lemuria for a long time, and we're pretty sure it's here.

BOOKSELLER: In this bookstore?

MAN: Yes. We've been tracking the energy for years and we're certain it's in a bookstore in Lincoln City. We're pretty sure it's this one, but it's possible it could be in a bookstore a few miles away.

WOMAN: No. Everything indicates that it should be here. Maybe under the stairs.

BOOKSELLER: Right. Well, have a look around, I suppose. Let me know if I can help you find anything!

Diana Portwood: *Bob's Beach Books, Lincoln City, Oregon, USA.*

(Teen daughter holds up a copy of The Canterbury Tales*)*
HER MOTHER: You're not old enough to read that. I'm not old enough to read that!

Lauretta Nagel: *Constellation Books, Maryland, USA.*

CUSTOMER: Hello! I'm searching for a book. I'm not sure of the publishing house, but it's really great and I just have to read it again.
BOOKSELLER: Sure. What was the title of the book?
CUSTOMER: Well, the thing is, I don't really remember …
BOOKSELLER: OK, then how about the author? Maybe we can search for their work and find the one you're looking for?
CUSTOMER: I don't know his name.
BOOKSELLER: … Right.
CUSTOMER: But he was definitely European.
BOOKSELLER: … Ok.
CUSTOMER: And it was non-fiction. Some kind of study. Probably.
BOOKSELLER: Right.
CUSTOMER *(looking expectantly at the bookseller)*: Come on, you must know the book I mean!

Sevda Nesheva: *Sofia International Book Fair, Bulgaria.*

CUSTOMER: Do you have the new Lady Gaga book by Terry Pratchett?
BOOKSELLER: ...

Caron McGarvey: *Waterstones, Glasgow, UK.*

CUSTOMER: I'm looking for the book *Mini Alcoholic* by Sophie Kinsella.

Joseph Segaran: *Waterstones, Amsterdam, The Netherlands.*

CUSTOMER *(on the phone)*: Hi. Do you sell drumsticks?
BOOKSELLER: Umm …the kind you eat or the ones you play drums with?
CUSTOMER *(eagerly)*: The ones you play drums with. Does that mean you carry them?
BOOKSELLER: No, I'm sorry; we don't have either. I was just curious to know which type you thought a bookshop might have. Try the music shop a couple of miles up the road.

Emily Crowe: *Odyssey Bookshop, South Hadley, Massachusetts, USA.*

(Customer holds up Fifty Shades of Grey *and shows her boyfriend)*
CUSTOMER: Babe! It's the book I was telling you about! My sister reckons it's exactly like us!

CUSTOMER: Oh my gosh, you guys sell plays! Does anyone buy them since, like, TV was made?

Chloe Flockart: *Elizabeth's, Perth, Australia.*

CUSTOMER: Do you have any foreign language dictionaries?
BOOKSELLER: Yeah, we do. I'll take you to our language section.
CUSTOMER: Oh, awesome! I need a Latin dictionary for my Spanish class.
BOOKSELLER: … Are you sure you don't need a Spanish dictionary?
CUSTOMER: No, Latin. They don't speak Spanish in Latin America.

♦

CUSTOMER: Do you sell manuals for fully automatic weapons?
BOOKSELLER: I don't think so. I have some pricing guides for guns, but no manuals.
CUSTOMER: Well, a pricing guide isn't gonna help me hunt humans, is it? I need a detailed manual!
BOOKSELLER: …

Pamela Morris: *Books-A-Million, Auburn, Maine, USA.*

CUSTOMER *(walking into the shop, shouts out)*: Don't expect me to buy anything. I'm not a reader!
BOOKSELLER: …

YOUNG GIRL: Did you know that rats don't like to walk on tightropes?
BOOKSELLER: No, I didn't.
YOUNG GIRL: Yeah, I found out when I tried to make my rat walk on a tightrope and he scratched me.

MOTHER: If you want to buy a book you'll have to use your own money. I've bought you enough books already!
DAUGHTER: But I've read all those books!
MOTHER: Well then, maybe you should learn to read slower!

Patty Whitney: *Blind Dog Books, Seabrook, Washington, USA.*

CUSTOMER: Hi, I'm looking for a Bible for my mother but I'm not quite sure who the author is.

(Phone rings)
BOOKSELLER: Good Afternoon, this is Waterstones; how may I help you?
CUSTOMER: Is this Waterstones, the bookshop?
BOOKSELLER: Yes it is, sir.
CUSTOMER: Good. Are you in the book department?

Emma-Louise Elliott: *Waterstones, Bristol, UK.*

CUSTOMER: I think I'll take a copy of this book.
BOOKSELLER: Sure, would you like a bag for it?
CUSTOMER: First, can you please get me a fresh copy?
BOOKSELLER: I'm sorry, what?
CUSTOMER: A fresh copy of the book. You know, not the display copy.
BOOKSELLER: Is this one damaged?
CUSTOMER: No, I'd just like a fresh copy.
BOOKSELLER: Well, our store is so small that we only have one or two copies of most books. Just about everything is out on display. We just sell them right off the shelves and tables.
CUSTOMER: Are you kidding?
BOOKSELLER: … No.
CUSTOMER: Right. Well, I'll have to think about it, then.
(Customer walks off.)

Anne DeVault: *Over the Moon Bookstore &*
Artisan Gallery, Crozet, Virginia, USA.

(Man approaches bookseller and attempts to start a conversation with her about religion)
BOOKSELLER: I'm sorry, sir, but I try to make a point of not discussing religion with customers.
CUSTOMER: Oh. I just thought you seemed like a nice girl, and I don't want you to go to Hell.
BOOKSELLER: …

CUSTOMER: I called earlier about *Slaughterhouse Five* for my class?
BOOKSELLER: Yes. I have a copy here for you.
CUSTOMER: OK, thanks. What's your return policy?
BOOKSELLER: … Why?
CUSTOMER: Because I only need it for, like, a week.

Lillian Clark: *The Second Story, Laramie, Wyoming, USA.*

CUSTOMER: Can you mail books to the jail?
BOOKSELLER: Sure.
CUSTOMER: Great. Do you have a list of all your true crime books?

Cathy Allard: *Bayshore Books, Oconto, Wisconsin, USA.*

CUSTOMER: Do you have the new book by Charles Dickens?
BOOKSELLER: Well, he hasn't published anything since the nineteenth century …
CUSTOMER: The new one that Oprah's promoting.
BOOKSELLER: Oh. *A Tale of Two Cities*, yes, we have that.
CUSTOMER: Yeah. Like I said: the new one.

Jessica Aimee Johnson: *Barnes and Noble, Pittsburgh, Pennsylvania, USA.*

MAN: Do you have any books on cars?
LIBRARIAN: We have a couple of books on cars in our transport section: one on Minis and one on Porsches.
MAN *(opens the book on Minis and points to a vehicle)*: Where abouts is this car?
LIBRARIAN: The caption says that it's a photo of Sir Alexander Arnold Constantine Issigonis, the man who designed the Mini, standing with a Mini in a garage in Birmingham in the 70s.
MAN: Great. Can you get his address for me?
LIBRARIAN: Sorry?
MAN: His address. I want to buy that car!

Rachel Armstrong: *Burnley Libraries, Lancashire, UK.*

MOTHER *(showing a picture book to her daughter)*: Awwww, look at the cute kitty. And the little horsey. And the groundhog, too! Your daddy shoots those when they come into the garden, doesn't he?

Marika McCoola: *Odyssey Bookshop, Massachusetts, USA.*

CUSTOMER: I'm looking for the fourth *Fifty Shades of Grey* book.
BOOKSELLER: There are only three in the series.
CUSTOMER: No, there are four. I saw it in another shop yesterday. It's really big. It's called *Fifty Shades Trilogy*.
BOOKSELLER: … That's the box set.

CUSTOMER *(staring intently at the bookseller)*: Are you Mary Magdalene?
BOOKSELLER: No.
CUSTOMER: Are you sure?
BOOKSELLER: … I'm pretty sure.
CUSTOMER: Because you look like Mary Magdalene.
BOOKSELLER: …

Danae Huff: *Barnes & Noble, Columbus, Ohio, USA.*

CUSTOMER: Do you have any of those books on symbols and stuff?
BOOKSELLER: What type of symbols do you mean?
CUSTOMER: You know, like a horseshoe – which I know is good luck – but what I want to know is: what does it mean when someone puts a dead bird through my letterbox?
BOOKSELLER: … I think it means they don't like you.

Dave Newman: *Waterstones, Hastings, UK.*

CUSTOMER: Thanks for helping me find those books the other week! Here – I've brought you a cheese pasty.
BOOKSELLER: Erm … well, er, thanks!

Philippa Powell: *Waterstones, Godalming, UK.*

CUSTOMER: I'm looking for a book but I don't know much about it so this could be hard.

BOOKSELLER: OK.

MAN: The title is *The Immortal Life of Something Something Something* …

BOOKSELLER (and the two other booksellers at the desk, in unison): *Henrietta Lacks.*

MAN (smiling): Great, thanks. So, what is a hard question?

BOOKSELLER: A hard question is 'Do you have this book I saw six months ago? It's blue.' And it turns out the book they want is actually yellow, and we haven't had a copy in the store for the past three years.

Melissa Ward: *Barnes and Noble, Coralville, Iowa, USA.*

♦

CUSTOMER: I need to return this book on ghosts.

BOOKSELLER: Is there a problem with it?

CUSTOMER: Yes. It's haunted.

Susan Holland: *SmithBooks, Victoria, British Columbia, Canada.*

CUSTOMER *(approaching the desk with a £7.99 paperback)*: I'd love to buy this book … But there's really no point.
BOOKSELLER: What makes you say that?
CUSTOMER: I have no grandchildren. Who would I pass it down to in my will? These days I never buy anything without questioning posterity.

◆

CUSTOMER *(in an urgent whisper, having waited for the other customers to leave the shop)*: Hello. Is your name 'Bookish Becca'?
BOOKSELLER: No, I'm Sarah.
CUSTOMER: You're not the person I've been chatting to online?
BOOKSELLER: Not that I'm aware of … Did this lady say she'd meet you here?
CUSTOMER: No.
BOOKSELLER: Does she live near here?
CUSTOMER: I have no idea.
Bookseller: What made you think it might be me, then?
CUSTOMER: Well, you look, you know, 'bookish.'

◆

CUSTOMER: Thank God you're open. The cat has sprayed all over my reference books. Can you help?
BOOKSELLER: … With the books – or the cat?

CUSTOMER: *(having spent two hours reading the same book in the shop)*: This book's great. I think I'll buy it.
BOOKSELLER: Excellent. It's £8.99 please.
CUSTOMER: Wait – these books are for sale? I meant I was going to buy it in a bookshop.
BOOKSELLER: This IS a bookshop.
CUSTOMER: Really? I just thought it was a place you let people read your books in.

◆

LITTLE BOY: Does this bookshop make money?
BOOKSELLER: Excuse me?
LITTLE BOY: I said, does this bookshop make money? I bet it doesn't. It's a bit of a silly idea having a bookshop on a boat, isn't it?
BOOKSELLER: … A lot of people like it.
LITTLE BOY: What's your business model? Do you have a five year plan?
BOOKSELLER: …
LITTLE BOY: You really don't know what you're doing, do you?
BOOKSELLER: … I'm selling books!
LITTLE BOY: It's not going to make you a millionnaire, though, is it?
BOOKSELLER: Well, no, but—
LITTLE BOY: When I grow up, I'm going to be a millionnaire.
BOOKSELLER: Are you?
LITTLE BOY: Yes. I haven't decided how, yet … But it won't be from selling books on a boat!

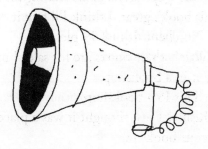

(on returning two weeks later)
LITTLE BOY: Hello. You still have no customers. If I owned this shop I'd fire you.
BOOKSELLER: Wow. Brutal. And then how would you proceed?
LITTLE BOY: I'd buy a megaphone and shout at people to buy my books. That's your problem – you don't shout at them.

CUSTOMER: I know I look like Saddam Hussein but, don't worry, I'm not him.
BOOKSELLER: It's OK. To my knowledge, he's dead. I wasn't too worried.
CUSTOMER: Really? Even with my moustache? You weren't even slightly panicked?
BOOKSELLER: … No.

Sarah Henshaw: *The Book Barge, Staffordshire, UK.*

CUSTOMER: Will you be getting Tolkien in for a signing soon?

BOOKSELLER: No, I don't think so.

CUSTOMER: Oh, that's a shame.

Kate Robotham: *Ottakers, Basingstoke, UK.*

LITTLE BOY: Excuse me, do you think this book will be too old for me?

CUSTOMER: Well, it depends how well you can read.

LITTLE BOY *(scornfully)*: Well, duh, I'm only three – I can't read at all!

Janet (via David) Hicks: *Bookstack, Berkhamsted, Hertfordshire, UK.*

CUSTOMER: I'm looking for a book called *Not Your Ordinary Average Day in the Park.*

BOOKSELLER: I'm not familiar with that one. Do you know what it's about?

CUSTOMER: It's about a boy with autism, and a dog.

BOOKSELLER: Do you mean *The Curious Incident of the Dog in the Night-time*?

CUSTOMER: Yes, that's it. I knew it had a title like that.

Josh Schasny: *Chapters Bookstore, Pointe-Claire, Montreal, Canada.*

CUSTOMER: Where are all of your paperbacks?
BOOKSELLER: All the books are in their specific sections, such as fiction, biography etc, organised by author.
CUSTOMER: You mean you don't separate the paperbacks from the hardcovers?
BOOKSELLER: No, only when they go on one of the New Release tables.
CUSTOMER: It's terrible that you just mix them in like that! I just can't believe it!

Ryan Dwyer: *Barnes and Noble, Lone Tree, Colorado, USA.*

CUSTOMER: Is this the only version of *Wolf Hall* that you've got?
BOOKSELLER: I'm sorry?
CUSTOMER: *Wolf Hall*, is this the only version?
BOOKSELLER: I'm sorry, I don't know of another version. I'm not really sure that I know what you mean, though.
CUSTOMER: It's far too long. I want the shorter version.
BOOKSELLER: I'm really sorry, but I don't think there is one.
CUSTOMER: Well, there must be. My neighbour says she's read it, and I know what she's like; she couldn't possibly have read anything that long.

CUSTOMER: It's a beautiful shop you have here.
BOOKSELLER: Oh, thank you.
CUSTOMER: It's just a shame that you filled it with all these ghastly books.

Hereward Corbett: *The Yellow-Lighted Bookshop,*
Nailsworth and Tetbury, UK.

CUSTOMER: Do you have copies of *Fifty Shades of Grey*?
BOOKSELLER: Yes, they're right over here. We don't have any secondhand ones in right now, though.
CUSTOMER: Oh, that's OK. I don't think I'd WANT a secondhand copy of that book, if you know what I mean! *(Customer and bookseller look at each other and burst out laughing)*

Stefani Kelley: *The Book Nook, Brenham, Texas, USA.*

CUSTOMER: If I had a bookstore, I'd make the mystery section really hard to find.

Anonymous

(Customer is doing push-ups in the middle of the bookstore. Lying beside him is an exercise book)
BOOKSELLER: Excuse me, sir, what are you doing?
CUSTOMER: I don't see why I can't practice the exercises first, before buying the book!

Anonymous

◆

(A couple approach the desk)
BOOKSELLER: Can I help you find something?
MAN: Yeah, we're looking for a vocabulary book. It's either called *The Soars* or *The Sars*.
BOOKSELLER: Let me look it up and see what we have.
WOMAN: Oh, it's OK; I made a note of the title.
(Customer pulls a napkin from her purse and lays it down for the bookseller to read. Written on it is: 'The Saurus.')

Anonymous

CUSTOMER: I'm looking for a book for my son. He's one of these weird people who still like the paper ones.

Anonymous

CHILD: Mom, how did Anne Frank escape the Nazis?
MOTHER: I'll tell you later.
CHILD *(screaming)*: BUT I WANT TO KNOW NOOOOOOWWW!
BOOKSELLER *(to fellow bookseller)*: Someone should tell her that she kept away from the Nazis for so long by being quiet.

Anonymous

(Phone rings)
BOOKSELLER: Thanks for calling Barnes and Noble, how can I help you?
CUSTOMER: Yeah, hi, um … do you sell Scrabble dictionaries?
BOOKSELLER: Yes, of course. Do you want me to put one on hold for you?
CUSTOMER: Oh, no that's OK. But, listen, I'm about to win this round, can you check to see if 'Kennedy' is included?

Anonymous

CUSTOMER: Hi. I'm looking for a stuffed animal.
BOOKSELLER: I'm afraid we don't really have any of those. We do have some books for babies, though. They're over here.
CUSTOMER: Er, it's for a B-A-B-Y. What's wrong with you? Babies can't read!

Anonymous

◆

(Customer is scraping his shoe along one of the display tables)
BOOKSELLER: Sir, please don't do that; you're making the table dirty.
CUSTOMER: But where else do you expect me to scrape this gum off my shoe?

Anonymous

◆

CUSTOMER: I've got a lot of books that I want to look through, so I've ordered a pizza to eat while I do that. Should I have them deliver it straight to the second floor, or should I meet them at the front desk?

Anonymous

MAN: Do you have a rest room?
BOOKSELLER: No, I'm afraid we don't.
MAN: Well, then, I'm peeing right here. *(He does so.)*

Anonymous

CUSTOMER: Do you have any books on flying?
BOOKSELLER: Sure, the aviation section is right over here.
CUSTOMER: No, man, I can already levitate; I need to know how to fly.
BOOKSELLER: You can levitate?
CUSTOMER: I'm doing it right now. My shoes are hollow, so it looks like I'm standing on the ground.

Anonymous

CUSTOMER: Do you … um … pay, like, more for signed books?
BOOKSELLER: For some books, yes, a signed copy would certainly be worth more.
CUSTOMER: What would you give me for … um … like, a signed copy of, like … *The Diary of Anne Frank*?
BOOKSELLER: I would give you something like a billion dollars for that.
CUSTOMER: Oh, awesome!

(It's just after 6pm. There's a sign on the desk asking the customers to ring the bell if a bookseller isn't at the till. A man rings the bell. The bookseller comes out from the back room.)
MAN *(looking from the bookseller to the bell in his hand)*: Wow. Just like in a brothel!

Nina Grahmann: *Thalia Bookshop, Europa Passage, Hamburg, Germany.*

CUSTOMER: You do have a lot of books, don't you?
BOOKSELLER *(gently)*: Well, it *is* a bookshop.

Susan Edgar: *Magill Book Exchange, St Morris, Australia.*

CUSTOMER *(angrily)*: I want to return this *Great Speeches in History* audiobook. It's not read by the original speakers! *(Speeches include those by George Washington, Abraham Lincoln & Julius Caesar.)*

Marc Murray: *Borders, Bondi Junction, New South Wales, Australia.*

CUSTOMER: Do you have that play by Hitler?
BOOKSELLER: ...
CUSTOMER: It's called *Titus Andronicus*. Apparently everyone dies.

(Two girls wander through the Medical section and find a copy of Gray's Anatomy*)*
GIRL: Oh God, I can't believe they named that book after the TV show ... They'll do anything to get people to buy books these days!
HER FRIEND: Yeah. That's so, so sad.

Claire Fitzgerald: *John Smith's Bookshop,*
Aras Na Mac Leinn, University College Cork, Ireland.

♦

CUSTOMER: I'm looking for a book. I think it'll be in fiction.
BOOKSELLER: Sure, fiction's in the big room on the first floor.
CUSTOMER: Just to check: is fiction the one that's true or the one that's not?
BOOKSELLER: ...

Ilona Gill: *Waterstones, Manchester, UK.*

CUSTOMER: Do you have *Pride and Produce*?
BOOKSELLER: Erm … Is that a cookbook?
CUSTOMER: No.
BOOKSELLER: A gardening book?
CUSTOMER: No.
BOOKSELLER: … Is it a novel?
CUSTOMER: Yes.
BOOKSELLER: Could you mean *Pride and Prejudice*?
CUSTOMER: Yes!

Rosie Phenix-Walker: *Blackwell's, Edinburgh, UK.*

◆

CUSTOMER: Where in the book does it tell you how many pages there are?

◆

CUSTOMER: Do you have that new book by that guy … I think his last name is Lama?
BOOKSELLER: Umm, the Dalai Lama?

◆

CUSTOMER: I'm looking for that magazine – the one that comes out every other month or so.

CUSTOMER: Do you have any books about absinthe? You know, the stuff that Picasso was drinking before he cut his ear off?

CUSTOMER: Where is your section for outdoor adventure literature?
BOOKSELLER: Are you looking for fiction or non-fiction?
CUSTOMER: Are those my only options?

Kimberly Dotson and the staff of *B. Dalton Booksellers, Manchester, New Hampshire, USA.*

CUSTOMER: Hi. Have you got a book on medicine for my sick Belgian pigeon?

CUSTOMER: May I bring the book back if the person I am buying it for is dead?

Carol Wright: *Wordsworth Books, Somerset West, South Africa.*

CUSTOMER: You haven't read *Fifty Shades of Grey*?
BOOKSELLER: No, I haven't.
CUSTOMER: I'd like to talk to someone who knows about books. *(Turns to another bookseller)* Do you know a lot about books? Do you read?

Roxanne Pena: *Barnes and Noble, Long Beach, California, USA.*

CUSTOMER ONE *(admiring a leather-bound classic)*: Wow, what a beautiful cover
CUSTOMER TWO *(while purchasing* Reflected in You *by Sylvia Day)*: I don't buy books because they're beautiful; I buy them because they expand my knowledge.

The booksellers of *Love That Book, Westfield Shopping Centre, Helensvale, Queensland, Australia.*

CUSTOMER: What is the first name of the author Anonymous?

Nicole Adams: *Jess Hann Branch, Oshawa Public Libraries, Oshawa, Canada.*

CUSTOMER: Do you sell cake plates?

CUSTOMER *(pointing at the fiction section)*: How are these books arranged?
BOOKSELLER: They're alphabetical.
CUSTOMER: By what? Title?
BOOKSELLER: No, by the author's name.
CUSTOMER: Their first name, or …
BOOKSELLER: Their surname.
CUSTOMER *(rolls his eyes)*: Christ. It's different in every bookshop, isn't it?

Kirsty Logan: *Ottakars, Buchanan Galleries, Glasgow, UK.*

CUSTOMER: I can't remember the title of the book I want but it's about a nurse.
BOOKSELLER: Is it fiction?
CUSTOMER *(with a look of disdain)*: Uh, no. It's a story.

♦

CUSTOMER: I wonder if you can help me. Where can I buy the pasta on the front of Nigella's book?

The booksellers of *Village Books, Wandsworth Common and Dulwich Village, London, UK.*

CUSTOMER: Do you have a large print Bible on cassette? My mom's hard of hearing.

Steve Laube: *A Christian Bookstore, Phoenix, Arizona, USA.*

CUSTOMER: Have you heard that nuclear weapons are a myth?

Chris Howard: *HCB Wholesalers, Hay-on-Wye, Powys, UK.*

CUSTOMER: I'm looking for a copy of *Tess of the d'Urbervilles* by Hardy. It was mentioned in *Fifty Shades of Grey* and I really liked that so I thought I'd give it a go.

Will, Colm, Kevin & Sinead: *The Campus Bookshop, UCD Dublin, Ireland.*

CUSTOMER: I need to change the name on my library card. *(Presents Deed Poll notification.)* I've changed my name to Michael Jackson for, you know, obvious reasons.
LIBRARIAN: ...

Steven Hartshorne: *Bolton Central Library, Bolton, UK.*

(The phone rings)

BOOKSELLER: Hello?

MAN: Hey! So, I just watched this movie and it said it was based on a true story, so I was wondering if there was a book to go with it?

BOOKSELLER: OK, sure, what was the movie?

MAN: *Battleship*. You know, the one with Rihanna. I really like Rihanna.

BOOKSELLER: Um, yeah … I'm sure I could find a sci-fi novel or other merchandise for you.

MAN: No, I want a historical or biographical book.

BOOKSELLER: I could find you something about battleships …

MAN: No, I want the true story of *Battleship* – with Rihanna.

BOOKSELLER: That movie is based on the board game, *Battleship*.

MAN: Uh, well, I just watched it and it's really good and it really happened.

BOOKSELLER: I haven't seen the movie, but isn't it about aliens attacking the Navy or something?

MAN *(enthusiastically)*: Yeah, exactly.

BOOKSELLER: …

Becca Perry: *Barnes and Noble, New England, Massachusetts, USA.*

CUSTOMER: I've been using the library a lot in the last six months to take out books about losing weight … You should, too!

Susie Kerr: *East Grinstead Library, West Sussex, UK.*

CUSTOMER: Do you have that book by that guy, the one whose brother is on the radio and has a moustache? I think it's blue.

BOOKSELLER *(jokingly)*: The moustache?

CUSTOMER *(seriously)*: No. The book.

◆

CUSTOMER: Do you have a book that will teach my dog how to speak English? … Or French. Either will do.

Hellen Mani: *Collins Booksellers, Moonee Ponds, Melbourne, Australia.*

◆

CUSTOMER: I'm looking for a book about the Holocaust; my daughter's very interested in World War II. But I don't want it to be a sad book.

BOOKSELLER: … Not a sad one?

CUSTOMER: No. No sad bits at all.

Madeleine Dowd: *Gertrude & Alice Cafe Bookstore, Bondi Beach, Australia.*

CUSTOMER: When is your next Book Club?
BOOKSELLER: In two weeks. *(Hands over a flyer.)* Here are the details. You're welcome to come along.
CUSTOMER: Oh good, and what will you be doing?
BOOKSELLER: We have a group discussion about the book nominated that month. It's all a bit of fun.
CUSTOMER: Ah. OK.
BOOKSELLER: Did you want a copy of this month's book?
CUSTOMER: Oh no. I don't read books.

Katherine FitzHywel: *The Grumpy Swimmer Bookshop,*
Melbourne, Australia.

CUSTOMER: Hi, I'm looking for a bookshop that sells antique door handles.

BOOKSELLER: Would you like a bag?
FRENCH CUSTOMER: No no no no.
(Pause.)
FRENCH CUSTOMER: Can I have a little baguette?

♦

CUSTOMER: Do you have Harry Potter's wand?

Tom Smith: *Waterstones, Amsterdam, The Netherlands.*

CUSTOMER: I'm looking for *The Blonde Assassin*.
BOOKSELLER: Do you mean *The Blind Assassin* by Margaret Atwood?
CUSTOMER: No, she's blonde, I'm sure!

◆

FRENCH CUSTOMER: I'm looking for a book by Marten Toonder.
BOOKSELLER: Is he a Dutch author?
FRENCH CUSTOMER: No, no – he is Hollandaise.

◆

BOOKSELLER: Hi, can I help you?
CUSTOMER: I'm looking for my friend; he's supposed to be at The English Bookshop. Are you The English Bookshop?
BOOKSELLER: We are *an* English bookshop.
CUSTOMER: Then why is my friend not here?

Anne Van Dam: *Waterstones, Amsterdam, The Netherlands.*

◆

CUSTOMER *(pushes in front of a long queue to the service counter, where a bookseller is clearly helping another customer, and asks)*: Where are your books on etiquette?

Camille Minor: *Borders, Melbourne, Australia.*

Weird Things Customers Say at *Weird Things Customers Say in Bookshops* Book Signings

Standing in a bookshop with copies of *Weird Things ...* to sign was bound to get a few strange looks, and perhaps confuse a couple of people, but I think I underestimated the irony of me going into bookshops, with *Weird Things Customers Say in Bookshops*, and interacting with the customers ...

♦

WOMAN: So. Are you the new J. K. Rowling, then? … You don't look like her. You've got different hair.

WOMAN: Can you tell me where the children's section is?
ME: I'm afraid I don't work here – I'm just here signing books today.
WOMAN: Oh. Well, what use is that?!

MAN: *Weird Things Customers Say in Bookshops* by Jen Campbell?
ME: Yep.
MAN: You wrote this?
ME: I did.
MAN: Cool. What's your name?
ME: … Jen Campbell.
MAN *(seriously)*: And what's the book about? Is it a thriller or something? Does it have vampires? I love vampires.

CUSTOMER: I recognise you. Were you on television?

ME: Nope, not that I'm aware of.

CUSTOMER: You were! I've seen you.

ME: I don't think so. I'm a writer.

CUSTOMER: Oh. Wait. Are there secret cameras here? Is this a fly-on-the-wall documentary?

ME: ... No. I'm, er, just signing books.

CUSTOMER: Well, you would say that, wouldn't you? Hmmm. Wait a minute, I'm just going to nip to the bathroom and do my make up. Then I'll come back and we can have this conversation again.

♦

CUSTOMER: All writers are millionaires, aren't they?

ME: Nope.

CUSTOMER: How much do you earn, then?

WOMAN *(walks up to me, holding up a copy of* Fifty Shades of Grey*)*: Will you sign this for me?

ME: ... I didn't write that book.

WOMAN: But the sign here says that you're signing books today.

ME: Yes ... I'm signing the book that I wrote *(indicates* Weird Things ...*)*

WOMAN: Just that one?

ME: ... Yes.

WOMAN: Not any of the others?

ME: ... No.

WOMAN: Oh, well, that's very odd. *(She wanders off, looking confused.)*

♦

MAN: *Weird Things,* ey?

ME: Yep.

MAN: You should follow my wife around; she says stupid things all the time.

ME: Really?

MAN: Yeah. Not necessarily in bookshops, just in life.

ME: Oh.

MAN: Yeah. Like, she tells people that I poisoned our cat. But I totally didn't.

ACKNOWLEDGEMENTS

Much love and thanks to Charlie and Hugh, and the lovely people at Constable and Robinson, and Ed Victor.

Love and thanks also to the marvellous Greg and his fantastic illustrations.

Thank you to all the booksellers and librarians who sent in quotes for this book, and a big hello to all the booksellers I've met whilst promoting *Weird Things* ... It's been wonderful visiting so many different bookshops, and chatting to so many great people. Long live bricks and mortar bookshops!

Lots of love and thanks to my excellent family and friends (especially Miles).